# 101 THINGS WOMEN CAN FINALLY DO AT 60

# HAPPY

# 60th

# BIRTHDAY

**FROM:** _____

**TO:** _____

# WELCOME TO THE 60 CLUB!

Sixty! Some people say it's the new forty. Others see it as a major milestone. And honestly? Some of us still can't quite believe we've actually hit it. (Spoiler Alert: you have, and it looks pretty damn good on you.)

If you're holding this book, it means someone really cares about you and knows that a birthday this special deserves way more than just another card with regular wishes inside.

This isn't some boring self-help guide or one of those preachy motivational books that make you feel guilty about eating cookies for breakfast. This is a collection of small joys, gentle rebellions, bold truths, and those long-overdue freedoms you've been secretly craving.
Inside these pages, you'll find 101 things you can—and absolutely should—do right now. Because here's the thing: at 30, you were busy building your life. At 40, you were managing everything and everyone. But at 60? Girl, it's time to fully enjoy the amazing woman you've become.

But first, let's have some fun and figure out if you're really ready for this club.

Are You Actually 60?
Here's a completely unscientific but totally accurate checklist to find out. Just check off each "symptom" that sounds like you. The more you nod along, the more you'll know you're exactly where you're meant to be.

Ready?
Let's kick things off with a smile, because that's how all the best things in life should start.

# YOU KNOW YOU'RE 60 IF...

Check off every circle that sounds like you
(and no cheating!)

○ You need to either hold labels far away, pull them super close, or just ask someone under 30 to read them for you.

○ Your knees crack more than your grandma's old wooden floors.

○ Your idea of the perfect Saturday night? Pajamas, couch, and blessed silence.

○ You catch yourself judging today's youth: their music, their clothes, and their behavior.

○ You talk to your plants. And yes, you actually listen to their responses.

○ You get more messages from group chats called "Moms Something" than from actual friends.

○ A new memory foam pillow excites you more than a new pair of shoes.

- ⚪ Mess up a text? No problem, just delete the whole thing and call instead.

- ⚪ When your hairdresser suggests "something new," you look at them like they just asked you to jump out of a plane.

- ⚪ One glass of wine reminds you – you're not 30 anymore.

- ⚪ Forget where your phone is? You're holding it.

- ⚪ You send only voice notes – long ones – with full commentary.

## YOUR FINAL SCORE:

**0–3 points:**
Wow! Are you sure you're actually 60? Either you totally cheated on this quiz, or you've found the fountain of youth. Either way, we're seriously impressed!

**4–8 points:**
You're enjoying all the best parts of this age without going full grumpy grandma. Nice work!»

**9 or more points:**
Congratulations, you've officially joined the 60 Club! Time to grab those reading glasses, start giving unsolicited advice, and enjoy those well-earned afternoon naps.

# 101 THINGS WOMEN CAN FINALLY DO AT 60

# ALWAYS REPLY WITH A VOICE MESSAGE. ALWAYS.

Texting? Too much effort. Typing with your glasses sliding down your nose? No thanks.
At 60, you've discovered real luxury: voice notes.

One to say thanks, one to explain why you're not going out tonight, one to recap the entire movie you just watched in under three minutes. One for every mood.

Let's be real—it's way easier to talk than to type. And nothing beats tone of voice, dramatic pauses, or sudden bursts of laughter. No emoji can capture that. And if someone complains about how long it is? Just send another one:
"Sorry, I wasn't done."

## 💡 BONUS TIP

If you swipe up while holding the mic, the recording locks and plays automatically—no need to keep pressing. Voilà: long, heartfelt monologues with one hand (and the other free for ice cream). Genius, right?

# CHOOSING WHO TO GO OUT WITH (AND WHO NOT TO) WITHOUT FEELING GUILTY

At 60, you're done wasting time on people who drain your energy.

The "obligation" hangouts? Over. Dinners with people who only talk about themselves? Over. Two-hour coffees that leave you feeling empty? Nope.

Now, you go out only with those who make you feel good. The ones who laugh with you, really listen, don't count calories on the plate, and never make you feel bad for talking too much—or not enough.

It's your new rule: zero social obligations, 100% honest choices.

It's not being picky. It's finally having the courage to protect your vibe.

## SAYING "AT MY AGE?" ... AND DOING IT ANYWAY

"At my age, can I really wear glitter?
"At my age, is it still okay to dance on tables?"
"At my age, isn't taking selfies a little ridiculous?"

Here's the right answer: Yes, at your age, you absolutely can.

In fact, this is the perfect time to not care what anyone thinks.

At 60, you've done all the things you were "supposed" to do—be serious, balanced, and responsible. Now, you get to be light, spontaneous, and a little wild—just for the joy of surprising the people who thought you were all "settled."

The truth is, that little voice asking, "At my age?" is just asking for permission.

And at 60, you don't need permission from anyone.

# CHANGING YOUR HAIR COLOR AT 60? IT'S LIKE ADDING A NEW CHAPTER TO YOUR STORY

It used to be about "covering the grays." Now, it's more like, "Today I feel copper red; tomorrow maybe cosmic silver."

At 60, hair dye isn't a chore–it's a chance to play. It's power, freedom, and a bold, "I do what I want." Whether it's highlighted, violet tones, or a platinum blonde that would make Aunt Mary clutch her pearls –the truth is, you can do whatever feels right.

Because at this age, you're not trying to look younger. You're just showing who you are today–with more style, more story, and (finally) more volume.

# CAREFULLY CHOOSING A MOVIE... AND FALLING ASLEEP AFTER THE OPENING CREDITS

You spend half an hour scrolling through Netflix.
You read the summaries, watch the trailers, and assess the cast.

You finally pick the perfect film, snuggle up with a cozy blanket, and dim the lights just enough to set the perfect mood.
Two minutes later... you're snoring like a well-fed cat.
At 60, the real entertainment is the intention.
You don't have to finish the movie to enjoy it.
In fact, sometimes falling asleep five minutes in is the clearest sign that you've finally found peace.
And the best part? Tomorrow, you'll do it all over again.

With the same movie.
Which you'll never finish. And that's perfectly fine.

## 💡 BONUS TIP

Set your TV to auto-turn off after 20 minutes.
That way, when you fall asleep (spoiler alert: you will), you won't wake up at 2 a.m. to the end credits of a Scandinavian thriller and your cat staring at you like something's wrong.

# FORGETTING WHY YOU WALKED INTO A ROOM

You get up, walk with purpose, enter the kitchen...
Then stop.

You look around, like a detective in a crime scene.
Then ask yourself, "Why did I come in here?"
Welcome to the club.
At 60, memory isn't like a Google search– it's more like a treasure hunt.

Sometimes, you win; other times, you have to retrace your steps and hope your brain switches back on.
But you don't get frustrated anymore. You just sit down, take a sip of water, and say:
"It's fine. If it's important, it'll come back."
And if it doesn't?
Oh well. Maybe it was something silly. Or a bill.

# CHOOSING WHO TO SPEND TIME WITH BASED ON COMPATIBLE LEVELS OF CRAZY

At 60, you're over polite, small talk that leaves you feeling like a shell of your former self.

You want friends you can laugh until you snort with, talk way too loud with, make up stories about squirrels ruling the city with, and critique random strangers' outfits like you're on "What Not to Wear." Balance? Overrated.

What you really need are people who get that crazy is a lifestyle, not a phase. If a friend suggests, "Let's pretend we're tourists downtown," and you reply, "Hold on, let me switch accents," you know you've found your tribe.

# YOUR YEAR OF BIRTH? A MYSTERY... WITH A TOUCH OF STYLE.

At 60, you don't lie—you deflect with charm.
Because your age isn't a secret...
it's just irrelevant.

You've got the energy of a forty-something, the patience of a sixty-something, and the boldness of someone who's finally learned to love herself. And no, you don't owe anyone an explanation.

Anyone really paying attention knows—you're not from a year.
You're from an era. Your own.

## 💡 BONUS TIP

When someone pushes too hard, just smile and say: "I honestly don't remember. I stopped counting when I started liking the number."

# NEVER TELL THE TRUTH ABOUT YOUR HAIR COLOR!

"What a gorgeous color! Is it natural?"
"Of course—just like my love for chocolate."
You smile, change the subject, and let them wonder.
At 60, the truth about your hair color is a completely irrelevant detail.

You've tried sun-kissed blondes, rich brunettes, bold reds—and yes, maybe even a pastel moment.
Each shade tells part of your story, but none of them define you.

And if someone presses?
Just answer with a wink:
"My stylist knows... but they're bound by client confidentiality."

# NOT CHASING A CAREER, CHASING PEACE. WITH YOURSELF.

You used to go after titles, promotions, and praise.
Climbing, rushing, proving.
At 60, you pause. You listen.
And you realize the biggest promotion is the one you give yourself: "I'm good now."
It's not apathy–it's clarity.

It's not giving up–it's winning.
You've learned that your life isn't a résumé.
You don't need to earn approval anymore.
You just need to see your own worth–even on the days when the only thing you accomplish is peace.
You're not less ambitious.

You've just changed your goal: serenity.

# LEAVING THE LAUNDRY IN THE WASHER WITHOUT A SENSE OF URGENCY

You used to rush the second the cycle ended.
Now, the laundry can stay right there. Resting. Reflecting.

You hear it, but you don't reply.
Has it been done for four hours? Perfect. That's a great time to keep ignoring it.
At 60, you realize nothing bad happens if the clothes sit there overnight. Or two.
You rewash them. Or shake them out. Or leave them until the machine folds them itself.

(Spoiler alert: it won't. But that's not your problem.)
You've learned that time isn't for things you have to do—it's for what you choose to do.
And today, guess what? You didn't choose the laundry.

## 💡 BONUS TIP

When the thought "Oh no, I have to hang the laundry!" pops up, smile and tell yourself:
"Actually, no." Then, go back to doing something truly urgent—like absolutely nothing.

# BUYING A NEW PLANNER IN OCTOBER JUST BECAUSE IT'S PRETTY

You don't need it. You've got your phone, the shared calendar, three Post-its on the fridge, and a mental system worthy of NASA.

But then you see it: hardcover, lined pages, maybe even gold details. And you tell yourself,
"This year, I'm going to be super organized."
Never mind that there are only two months left in the year.

You buy it anyway.
Because you feel like it. Because it's pretty. Because it's yours.
And maybe you'll actually use it... to jot down motivational quotes, shopping lists, or to-do's that never get done.
But still—every time you look at it, you feel like a woman with a plan.
And that's already a win.

# READING A MESSAGE. THINKING ABOUT IT. NOT REPLYING. PERIOD.

It used to be: "I have to reply right away, or I'll seem rude."
Now it's: "I'll read it. Think about it. Maybe I'll reply. Maybe not. We'll see."

At 60, you don't chase beeps, chats, or other people's urgency anymore.
You've learned that not everything deserves your time—right now.
You've got other priorities: breathing, picking a movie, reheating your tea for the fourth
time, staring out the window.

Replying is a choice, not an obligation.
And whoever's texting you can learn one thing:
You're not a vending machine for answers.

# BUYING YET ANOTHER "MIRACLE" CREAM... AND FORGETTING IT IN A DRAWER

You've got your day cream, night cream, eye cream, the one with acid, the one with retinol, and the one you're only supposed to use on odd-numbered months during a waxing moon.

And yet, every time you walk into a beauty store and see "visible lifting in 7 days,"... you fall for it. Proudly.

Because at 60, you're not buying cream just for your skin.

You're buying it for the illusion. For the scent. For the chic little jar.

And for that quiet moment in front of the mirror when you treat yourself like the most precious thing you own.

(Spoiler alert: you are.)

Then maybe you forget to use it. Or you try it for two days before it joins the plumping night mask in drawer purgatory.

That's perfectly fine.

Even your bathroom drawer deserves to dream.

# TALKING TO ALEXA LIKE SHE'S YOUR ROOMMATE

At 60, you start talking to yourself—but with style: through Alexa.
"Alexa, what's the weather tomorrow?"
"Alexa, play something relaxing."
"Alexa, turn off the lights... and maybe my thoughts, too, if you can."

You even say "thank you," even though you know she doesn't care.
Sometimes, you ask her things just to feel less alone in the kitchen. Other times, you argue like she's a real person:
"Not that volume, Alexa! Are you kidding me right now?"

And if one day you catch yourself telling her about your dreams from last night... Well, it's official—she lives with you.

# SAYING "I DON'T FEEL LIKE IT" AND LETTING THAT BE A COMPLETE ANSWER

You used to come up with creative excuses: "Oh, sorry, I have plans." "I can't, today's crazy."
Now? You've perfected the art of the ultimate power move: "I don't feel like it."

No explanations. No, "maybe next time." Just no.
It's not rude—it's truth at its finest. It's the end of fake stomach bugs, imaginary cousins, and last-minute "I've got another call" lies.
It's about respecting your time, your energy, and your couch.

The people who care about you will get it.
The ones who push? Deserve a graceful "maybe another time," delivered in your best Meryl Streep voice.

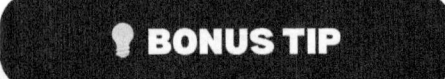

If they ask, "Why not?" just shrug and say: "It's my emotional day off. I'll be back tomorrow—maybe."

# GOING TO THE GROCERY STORE LIKE IT'S A RUNWAY

**16**

At 60, grocery shopping isn't just a chore—it's a ritual of independence.
You glide through the aisles like you're starring in your fashion show, swiping that avocado like you've been cast as the lead.

Those 20-somethings trying to read the label on the milk? You smile because you already know what's going on in your cart—extra cheese, two bottles of wine, and cookies "for the grandkids" (who are probably too young to notice that you've eaten half of them before they arrive).
And if you leave with your hair in a messy bun, glasses slipping down your nose, and a purse that's so full it could double as a suitcase?
Don't sweat it. You've got that "I'm winning at life" look down.

# CARRYING A BAG THAT HAS EVERYTHING... EXCEPT WHAT YOU'RE LOOKING FOR

Your purse is more than an accessory. It's like a bottomless pit of "What's that thing called again?"

Lipstick, reading glasses, tissues, old receipts, half-eaten mints... you've got it all. And let's be real: you've got four pairs of glasses in there, but none are the right prescription.

So, when someone says, "Wow, your bag is heavy," just smile and reply, "It's a life well lived."
And if you're lucky enough to actually find what you're looking for in there? Consider it a treasure hunt victory. Besides, it's good to be ready for anything. From sudden rain to a friend's midlife meltdown.

After all, if Mary Poppins had a flying umbrella, you're allowed to carry three wallets and a coffee spoon "just in case."

# SAYING WHAT YOU THINK. IN YOUR WORDS. WITH WHATEVER FACE YOU WANT.

At 60, you stop nodding just to be polite, stop smiling to soften the truth, and stop sending emojis to cushion your messages.

Now, if something's on your mind, it's coming out— whether you've got a filter or not.

Someone bores you? You change the subject.

Your dress makes you look like a million bucks? You buy it.

It's not arrogance—it's efficiency. You've spent years softening your words for other people's feelings. Now? It's about your feelings.

The people who love you will appreciate your honesty. And the ones who get offended? Well, maybe they were just used to the version of you who said "maybe" when she really meant "no."

# PRETENDING NOT TO HEAR AND ENJOYING SELECTIVE SILENCE

"Did you hear what your mother-in-law said?"
"Did you see your cousin's recent Facebook post?"
"Someone needs to organize the neighborhood BBQ."

Huh? Sorry, I didn't quite hear that.
At 60, you've mastered the art of emotional hearing.
You hear everything, but only store what matters.
The rest? You just let it slide off like a bad song on the radio.

Pretending not to hear isn't rude—It's self-care. And when you've earned your peace, you've earned it in silence.

# TALKING TO PLANTS... BECAUSE AT LEAST THEY DON'T INTERRUPT

At 60, you talk to your plants.
You check in with them; are they thirsty? Do they need a little pep talk?

And let's face it: plants don't argue, they don't gossip, and they don't ask for a status update.
Sometimes, they're the only ones who truly listen.
And hey, if the orchid dies, it's not because it didn't try; it's just because sometimes plants, like people, have their moments of drama.

But let's be honest; on some days, the only real conversation you're up for is with your fern.

# ADMITTING YOU CAN'T SEE ANYMORE... AND LAUGHING ABOUT IT

One minute, you're reading everything just fine; the next, you're squinting at the shampoo bottle under your phone's flashlight.

Yep, it's official: the print has gotten smaller. Or maybe it's just marketing. (Let's go with that.)

At 60, you can finally stop pretending you see perfectly. You get to say, "I can't see a thing—send me screenshots in XXL," with zero shame. You can hold the menu up to the ceiling, looking for the perfect lighting, and laugh with those who get it.

It's not a weakness—it's a selective visual experience. You only focus on what deserves your attention, and the rest can stay blurry.

After all, you've spent a lifetime reading the fine print —bills, contracts, and tiny recipe cards. Now, if you can't read a label, you simply ignore it with style.

## 💡 BONUS TIP

Keep a magnifying glass in the kitchen and a pair of "battle glasses" in the living room. When someone teases you, just say, "Better not to see the wrinkles anyway, right?"

# USING YOUR KIDS AS AN EXCUSE... EVEN IF THEY'RE THIRTY

**23**

"I can't tonight; the kids need me."
Said with a serious tone, a knowing look, and maybe a little sigh.

No one has to know that "the kids" are 31, living on their own, and probably out having cocktails downtown while you're slipping on polka-dot socks for a glorious night on the couch.
At 60, you've earned the right to say no without an explanation. But if you want a classy excuse, mentioning your kids is a timeless go-to. They owe you their life—so let them help you gracefully decline invitations.

The truth is, after countless social nights, obligatory dinners, awkward birthday parties, and toasts with strangers; you've earned the sacred right to choose peace, quiet, and maybe even pajamas by 8 p.m.

# EATING ICE CREAM STRAIGHT FROM THE TUB (WITHOUT THE GUILT)

At 60, you're done pretending to be refined when it comes to dessert.

Truth is, you've earned the right to dig your spoon straight into the tub, in your pajamas, while watching a show you've already seen three times.
No more diet-sized scoops in tiny designer bowls. You want the ice cream—all of it—and if anyone dares to judge, just say it's preventive therapy for family-induced stress.

At this age, it's not "cheating"—it's celebrating the freedom to choose joy, especially when that joy is dark chocolate and salty hazelnut.
And the best part? No one can ask, "Are you sure?"—because yes, you are absolutely sure.

# LAUGHING OUT LOUD EVEN IF YOU PEE A LITTLE

At 60, you laugh deeper, wiser, and harder. You laugh at the absurd, the unexpected, and your own quirks— and sometimes, you laugh so hard that a little pee sneaks out.

So what? It comes with the territory. Real laughter hits the bladder, too.
It's not a tragedy—it's your body's way of saying, "Yep, you're alive!" You're joyful, you're present, and if a laugh surprises you... well, it's better than an unexpected bill.

So laugh it off—literally. Keep a good giggle on hand and a panty liner in your bag: humor is your new core workout.

# STRATEGICALLY IGNORING THE MESS... AND CALLING IT EMOTIONAL MINIMALISM

There's a lone sock on the chair?
A dish in the sink?
A pair of shoes that look abandoned for days?
At 60, you no longer feel the need to jump up and tidy up everything.

You think: "Not now. Maybe never."
You've learned to look past it.
You've realized true cleanliness is in your mind.
Homes may look great in magazines, but in reality, there's always a chair covered in clothes that are "not clean but not dirty."

Leave that everyday mess right where it is—it's not laziness; it's self-preservation.
And if someone drops by and raises an eyebrow, just smile and say:
"I'm making space. Inside and out."

## 💡 BONUS TIP

When the thought "Oh no, I should clean that!" pops up, sit down and ask yourself:
"Am I doing this for me... or to impress?"
If the answer doesn't excite you, get up—but only to walk into another room.

# TURNING OFF YOUR PHONE... AND FEELING YOUR BRAIN POWER BACK ON

There was a time when every ping made you jump.
Now, real luxury is silence.
That moment when you hold down the button and... click: black screen.

It's like closing a door, dimming the lights, and finally sitting down at home—inside yourself.
At 60, you no longer feel the need to reply right away or stay available to the entire world.
You've learned that if someone truly needs you... they can wait.

And if they can't? That's not your problem.
Turning off your phone isn't disappearing.
It's reappearing in your real life—the one with free thoughts, hot tea, and that show you've already spoiled for yourself... but still want to watch again.

# TAKING A BREAK FROM EVERYTHING... TO "WATCH JUST ONE EPISODE" (SPOILER: IT'LL BE FOUR)

You said just one–just to unwind.

Three hours later, you're still there, wrapped in a blanket, face tense with suspense, herbal tea long forgotten and purely symbolic.

At 60, TV series become a personal religion.

You have specific tastes, high narrative standards, and the sharp eye of a seasoned critic.

You'll endure slow plots, pointless characters, and awkward dialogue... but heaven help anyone who spoils something.

And no, it's not wasted time. It's horizontal therapy.

It's your way of not talking to anyone after dinner–and falling in love again, even if it's just with a detective and a tragic haircut.

# GOSSIPING WITH YOUR FRIENDS... LIKE IT'S A CIVIC DUTY

It's not gossip. It's data collection. Emotional updates. Collective mood management. At 60, the real recurring event is the women's catch-up: coffee, laughter, and a flood of useless details that somehow save your soul.

You talk about everyone: the too-perfect coworker, the ex with his new girlfriend ("young, but clearly freezing"), the woman who only posts motivational selfies at 6 a.m. No jealousy—just scientific observation.
Sometimes even educational: "I swear I'll never end up like that."
Because let's be honest: some chats with your girlfriends are worth more than ten therapy sessions, and only cost a cappuccino and half a croissant (shared—pretend).

# BOOKING A LAST-MINUTE TRIP WITH THE GIRLS

It all starts with one message:
"What if we just got away this weekend?"
Five minutes later, the flight's booked, the hotel's reserved, and there's a new group chat called "Escape from Reality."
At 60, a girls' trip isn't a wild idea–it's routine prevention.

You laugh like you haven't in months.
You talk for hours, never finishing a single story, and it doesn't matter.
You get lost in Google Maps and somehow end up with a drink in hand and tears in your eyes.
You don't need a tropical destination.

You just need the will to go. The joy of being together. And the beautiful reminder that you're still alive, still radiant, and still able to pack a bag in 10 minutes flat.

## 💡 BONUS TIP

To travel smart without breaking the bank, use apps like Hopper, Google Flights, or Amtrak to find the best weekend deals. Then book a cool stay on Airbnb and split the cost–just like college, but with better slippers and a shared Spotify playlist called "Hot Flash Getaway."

## CELEBRATING THE LITTLE DAILY WINS

Do you remember your Wi-Fi password on the first try?
Found a parking spot right in front without circling the block for 20 minutes?
Cooked something delicious without even glancing at a recipe?
You deserve a round of applause. Maybe even a toast.
At 60, a day without drama is a day well done.
You don't need grand milestones—just the ability to see magic in the small stuff.
And if no one's handing out compliments?
You give them to yourself.

Because some days, leaving the house on time, remembering your umbrella, and not
snapping at anyone...
is the real victory.

# DELETE ANYONE FROM YOUR CONTACTS WHO ONLY MESSAGES YOU ON CHRISTMAS, EASTER, AND NEW YEAR'S—WITH THE SAME OLD COPY-PASTE GREETINGS.

**32**

You know exactly who they are.

Radio silence for 11 months, then—like clockwork—they pop up with:

"Wishing you and your family a wonderful holiday season!"

Same words. Same emojis. Zero warmth.

By 60, you've learned that the wishes that matter aren't mass-produced. They come with your name, a quirky sentence, a shared memory.

You don't need a message "just because it's that time of year."

You'd rather get a random "thinking of you" on April 7 or September 21.

So, between a glass of wine and a bite of lasagna, scroll through your contacts and clean house.

Because the best gift you can give yourself is letting go of relationships that only exist as calendar reminders.

# BUY YOURSELF SOMETHING EXPENSIVE—WITHOUT ASKING ANYONE'S PERMISSION.

At 60, you've stopped making excuses.
You've stopped saying:
"It was just a little treat,"
"It was on sale,"
"I totally earned it" (even though it's absolutely true).
Now, you see something you love, check your account, take a breath...
and you buy it.
Period.
Whether it's a purse, a piece of jewelry, a dream weekend, or a chair that feels like a
hug—it's not a luxury; it's a statement.
"I matter. I'm worth it. I choose me."
And no, you don't need to run it by anyone.
You don't need approval.
If someone asks, "But did you really need it?" Just smile and say,
"No. But it makes me feel good."

# OWN YOUR "BOOMER" TITLE— AND BE PROUD OF IT. YOU LIVED THROUGH THE BEST OF TIMES.

At 60, being called a "boomer" might sound like an insult.

But you just smile and bask in the glory of your golden years.
You lived your days without having to reply to anyone every two minutes.
You loved, argued, laughed, and traveled—without posting about it.
You used payphones, wrote letters by hand, and recorded songs off the radio, praying the DJ wouldn't talk over the intro. The truth?

Your youth was real, slow, and full.
And you didn't need filters to feel pretty—just a dash of lipstick and your trusty Walkman.

**35**

## BUY YOURSELF FLOWERS.

There was a time you hoped someone else would give them to you.

Now, you walk into the flower shop, pick your favorites, and carry them home like a well-earned prize.

At 60, there's no need for a special occasion. You just want a little beauty in your life.

Love tulips? Grab 'em.

Daisies got your heart? Toss 'em in the kitchen.

Sunflowers that scream, "Look at ME!"? Yup, they're coming home with you.

And you're not looking for romance. You're just giving yourself some well-deserved love. Because the only one you're trying to impress now is YOU.

# SINGING AT THE TOP OF YOUR LUNGS IN THE CAR... AND FEELING BETTER THAN ANY THERAPY

**36**

At 60, your car becomes your personal stage.
Close the door, and the world's judgment lowers with the window.

You hit play on your favorite playlist (packed with songs you've known by heart for
twenty years), and boom—the concert begins.
Off-key? Absolutely.
Still singing at red lights next to a confused stranger? Without question.
Drumming the steering wheel like it's your drum kit? Always.

Because at 60, you've learned it's not about singing well—it's about singing loud.
And the freedom to belt out "Life! My love!" with zero shame is worth more than a thousand mindfulness sessions.

## 💡 BONUS TIP

Create an "emotional emergency playlist": only tracks that revive your soul by the first chorus. (Yes, include that tearjerker from the '90s. You know the one.)

# BOOKING A LAST-MINUTE WEEKEND—JUST YOU AND YOUR HUSBAND

One click, two light bags, and you're off.
No lists, no plans, no "What should I cook for Monday?"

Just you, him, and a booking made with love (and a decent online discount).
At 60, you don't need a special occasion to unplug.
It's less "vacation" and more "vay-cushion," because all you really need is a bed that's not your bed and the absence of any reminders about unpaid bills.

Whoever's looking for you—can wait.
Whoever loves you—will understand.
And whoever's home... can figure out the microwave.

# BEING IN THE YOGA MOMS' FACEBOOK MESSENGER CHAT... AND STILL NOT SURE IF IT'S ABOUT STRETCHING OR STEFANY

Every week, you walk into class thinking, "Time to relax." Then your phone buzzes:
"Hey, ladies, who's coming tomorrow?"
Before you know it, you're flooded with messages, calming GIFs, a few inspirational memes, and a passionate debate about the new salmon-pink yoga mat from Target.

At 60, you've learned that the real practice... is staying zen in the Messenger thread. Yoga might get a mention on Mondays, but the rest of the week, it's all about teenagers, hot flashes, gluten-free banana bread, and Stefania—who changed instructors because "his energy felt... stuck."
And yet, you stay.
Because, at some point, you've stopped questioning why it's a battle between avocado toast and Zen. You just smile and type, "Skipping class today—Mercury's messing with my vibe."

# DRIVING PAST A SCHOOL AND THINKING: "THANK GOD I DON'T HAVE TO DO THAT ANYMORE"— AND SMILING

It's 8:02 a.m.
Outside the school: traffic chaos, double-parked cars, oversized backpacks, sleep-deprived kids, and parents in camouflage pajamas. You watch it all unfold...

From your car window, with a hot coffee in hand and absolutely no obligations.
At 60, you no longer have to fight over mismatched socks, fill out endless forms, or attend a last-minute PTA meeting at 5:30 p.m. You're done.
You gave. You conquered.
And as you see that teary-eyed mom clutching a croissant, you think:

"Hang in there, sister. You've got this."
Then you turn up your favorite song... and drive away in peace.

# HOLDING HANDS WHILE YOU WALK—JUST LIKE YOU DID WHEN YOU WERE DATING

At sixty, some gestures shine with a whole new light. Walking hand in hand with your husband isn't just a sweet habit—it's a quiet ritual that
tells the story of years lived side by side.
You don't need a special occasion.
Just a peaceful stroll is enough to bring back that tenderness time has made even deeper.
Fingers intertwine; naturally, your steps fall into sync, and in that simple touch lives the memory of laughter, struggles, waiting, and shared dreams. It's no longer the impulsive gesture of your twenties.
It's something steadier, sweeter—a sign that you're still here. Together.
No words needed, no plans required.
The beauty is simply being there. Side by side.
Because even if the world keeps rushing ahead, you can give yourself the luxury of slowing down and enjoying the moment.
And that small act of holding hands becomes a quiet declaration:
"We're still us. And walking together still means everything."

## MIXING UP THE NAMES OF KIDS, GRANDKIDS, AND EVEN THE DOG... AND LAUGHING ABOUT IT

At 60, your brain is like a full file cabinet of names, faces, and memories. So yes, sometimes you call your son by your grandson's name, your grandson by the dog's, and– on rare occasions–the dog by your ex's.

But hey, it's not a mistake. It's just a little brain multitasking.

Experts call it "misnaming"–but you know it's just love trying to find the right label.

So next time you mix them up, just smile and say, "Whoops, I was feeling all of you."

### 💡 BONUS TIP

Give everyone sweet nicknames: "Honey," "Love," "Darling." That way, when you forget their name, no one notices–and everyone feels like a VIP.

# CLAIMING THAT "MENOPAUSE IS JUST A NEW SUPERPOWER"

Hot flashes? Superpower.
Mood swings that hit like an unexpected rollercoaster? Superpower.

Restless sleep, forgetfulness, and arguing with the fridge? Still superpowers—now with bonus night mode.
At 60, menopause doesn't creep in. No, it crashes through the door like a fabulous, high-maintenance friend who's determined to make you take up ALL the space.

You may not be able to find your keys, but you can find your voice.
Now, you say no without explaining, choose what feels good, stop pleasing everyone, and finally, start showing up for yourself.
Menopause isn't weakening; it's setting you free.

## GETTING IN THE CAR... AND FEELING LIKE THE QUEEN OF THE WORLD

At 60, driving isn't just "getting from A to B." –it's a mini vacation.

It's your private, mobile kingdom where no one can interrupt you, the playlist is on point, and the coffee cup holder actually holds your coffee (for once).
Traffic? Pffft. That's me-time to think, breathe, sing (badly), and question your life choices.
Missed a turn? Oh well–more time to re-evaluate your life direction.
Parking far? Built-in cardio and personal space.
The GPS telling you to "turn left in 600 feet?" Yeah, no. Mute, please.

At this age, even a quick grocery run feels like an act of independence.

# SAYING, "I DON'T NEED EXPLANATIONS, I'VE GOT EXPERIENCE"

At 60, you don't need to understand everything down to the last detail.
You get it with just a glance.
A tone. A pause. Maybe even just a sigh.
You've been there, done that, and have the emotional scars to prove it.

You can spot a well-dressed lie from a mile away, and you know when someone's calling just because they need something.
So when you say, "Something feels off, but don't ask me why," just know it's not hesitation—it's a diagnosis made entirely on instinct.

Anyone asking for an explanation? They simply haven't lived long enough yet.

# TURNING DOWN AN INVITE... AND ENJOYING EVERY SECOND OF NOT BEING THERE

Once upon a time, you said yes to everything: happy hours, dinners with distant cousins, and those "just because" parties you didn't want to attend.

At 60? "No thanks, I can't make it" is your new favorite phrase.
And deep down, you're relieved.

No outfit stress, no last-minute makeup application, no "how's work" small talk.
Just you, your pajamas, snacks, and the pure bliss of doing absolutely nothing.
FOMO? Gone. You've discovered the JOY OF NOT SHOWING UP.

And if you scroll through Instagram stories of people pretending to have fun?
You sip your wine, smile, and think, "I won. Big time."

# WEARING LIPSTICK JUST TO TAKE OUT THE TRASH

For years, you saved lipstick for "special occasions"– dinners, dates, meetings. Now, any excuse will do: taking out the trash, answering the door, waving at the delivery guy.

Because at 60, lipstick isn't for anyone else. It's for you. It's your "I like myself," your "today I choose me," your "look at this fabulous face, even when I'm just tossing out the recycling."
Fiery red, classy nude, bold fuchsia–there are no rules, just the joy of seeing yourself shine, even at home.

And if someone asks, "All that just to step outside for a second?" you can calmly answer:
"Because I can."

## 💡 BONUS TIP

Keep a lipstick in the key drawer. That way, even if you're rushing out to turn off the gas, you'll look exactly as you are–an urban legend with slightly smudged mascara... and flawless lips.

# LOOKING IN THE MIRROR... AND GREETING YOUR WRINKLES BY NAME

You see them. They're there. Some are new; some are old friends.

That one on the left? It showed up after a week of laughing till you cried.
The fine one above your brow? A gift from your teenager. The one by your mouth? Probably a little comma of joy.

At 60, there's no need to hide them, smooth them out, or blur them with filters. Wrinkles are the handwritten notes of your life story. They don't take anything away– they add depth.

And if someone asks, "Have you tried that miracle cream?" You can answer, "Yes. It's called experience."

# BUYING A CAKE AND SAYING IT'S "FOR A FRIEND" (SPOILER: IT'S YOU)

**48**

"It's for a birthday."
"There's a dinner tonight."
"It's just a little something for a friend."

Sure, sure. And somehow, the cake makes it home... and never leaves.
At 60, you don't need a reason to buy cake. Heck, you don't need a reason to eat it. Triple chocolate, frosted with a dash of caramelized hazelnuts, or the one that just says "Happy Birthday" because who doesn't love a little birthday spirit on a Wednesday?

The truth is, sometimes you just need cake. And if it happens to be "for a friend," well... no one's judging. The only question is: Do you need a spoon, or are you just diving in face-first?

Because at 60, you're not waiting for a celebration. Sometimes, the best reason to celebrate is you.

# POPPING OPEN A BOTTLE "JUST BECAUSE" EVEN IF IT'S TUESDAY

There was a time when wine was reserved for "special occasions."

Now? A Tuesday feels like a special occasion if you've managed to get out of bed and remember what day it is.

At 60, you don't need a perfect occasion—you are the occasion.

A chilled glass of white while you cook, a splash of red on the couch, a toast to yourself even if it's raining outside.

It's not about "drinking." It's about honoring the little moments that used to slip by unnoticed.

Like saying no to something you didn't feel like doing.

Or putting on lipstick for no reason.

Or making peace with the fact that dinner is... yogurt and crackers.

Wine is the new bookmark of the day: when it shows up, everything else can wait.

## ANSWERING "HOW OLD ARE YOU?" WITH A SMILE... AND A FRAME-WORTHY LINE

**50**

"How old are you?"
Oh, the age-old question. At 60, you've got a million answers, and they're all better than "I'm 60."

Today, you might say, "Old enough to know what I want, and too old to put up with dumb questions."
Tomorrow, try, "Just the right age to do whatever I want."

Or, "Take a guess. But be careful—if you guess too high, you'll regret it."
Because age? It's not just a number. It's your superpower, a badge of honor, a declaration of freedom.

And anyone asking? They're not ready for the plot twist.

# TAKING OFF YOUR BRA AT 6 P.M. AND FEELING LIKE A NEW WOMAN

The real luxury at 60? It's not a spa day.
It's when the bra comes off.

You don't wear one out of obligation anymore. You wear it if you want—and only if it feels like a soft hug, not an epic torture device.
That old "support" bra with the wires that could double as coat hangers? Gone. And if you happen to forget to wear one? No explanation needed. You've earned the freedom to make your own rules.

So, when the bra comes off at 6 p.m., it's not just about comfort—it's about reclaiming your life. No wires, no straps. Just you, breathing easy, and maybe even dancing around the kitchen in your pajamas. (Because why not?)

# BUYING THE GOOD WINE JUST FOR YOU

Remember when the fancy bottle of wine was reserved for guests, birthdays, or "special" occasions?

Yeah, at 60, the occasion is you.
All it takes is a decent glass, the right playlist, and that quiet sense that your time isn't being wasted anymore.

Sip slowly. Savor it.
Even if you're eating an omelet.
Even if it's Tuesday.
Even if you put on pajamas at 6:30 p.m.
That good wine is a reminder that you deserve the best—even with no witnesses.

## 💡 BONUS TIP

Write on the bottle cap:
"To open when I love myself."
Then open it immediately. Because, really, you've earned it. And yes, you can toast by yourself. You'll get it.

# GOING TO THE HAIRDRESSER TWICE A WEEK

**53**

One blowout on Monday to face the week with the energy of a caffeinated squirrel.

Another one on Friday, just to make sure you're ready to rule the weekend.

At 60, the hairdresser isn't just about looking good— it's emotional therapy wrapped in salon smells.
You don't just get styled; you get pampered, heard, and understood. If someone asks, "Weren't you just there?"

You smile and reply, "So what? My hair lives in the now."

# STARTING TO LOOK FORWARD TO RETIREMENT... EVEN IF IT'S IN 2047

**54**

You did the math. Then you did it again.
And then, you realize—retirement is more of a state of mind.

But still, the dreams are real. You're already picturing a slow dog, scenic slippers, endless coffee, and pajamas as your official work attire.
Sometimes, you even say it out loud, like a mantra:
"When I retire..."

And deep down, you already feel the relief—even if it's still 18 years, 7 months, and a few surprise policy changes away.
At 60, just imagining retirement is your well-earned right.
In fact, you might even call it meditation. The best kind.

# TAKING YOUR TIME... EVEN WHEN YOU DON'T HAVE TO

At 60, you've learned one essential truth:
Rushing doesn't make you more efficient. It just makes you anxious.

Now, you walk slower through the grocery store, read labels carefully, and pick fruit like you're adopting it.
And when someone says, "Come on, hurry up!" You smile—and slow down on purpose.

You've spent your whole life rushing—rushing for work, for the kids, for appointments.
Now, you decide when to speed up and when to pause in front of the discounted cookies.
(Most of the time, it's the latter.)

# CHANGING YOUR MIND. OFTEN. WITH EASE AND NO WARNING

"I'm going out!" → You stay home.
"I'm cutting my hair short!" → You book the appointment... then cancel it.

"This year, it's a mountain vacation!" → Two days later, you book the beach.
At 60, changing your mind isn't indecision–it's advanced flexibility.
You've stopped feeling obligated to follow through on every plan made in a moment of excitement or hunger.
Now you decide based on your mood, your energy, the weather... or even the moon phase, if needed.
The truth? You've earned the right to listen to yourself.

And if what you want today isn't what you wanted yesterday– even better.
You're alive. And up to date.

# WORRYING ABOUT YOUR KIDS EVEN IF THEY'RE 30... BECAUSE YOU'RE STILL THEIR MOM

At 60, your kids might have jobs, their own homes—maybe even kids of their own. But, spoiler alert: They'll always be "your babies."

- You call to check if they've eaten anything that's not microwaveable.
- You ask them to pack an umbrella... even if it's still sunny.
- You panic when they don't reply to your text within an hour.

And when they say, "Mom, I'm fine, really," you smile and think, "Oh honey, I've been fine before. But I'm still calling."

### 💡 BONUS TIP

When you feel like you're a tad too present, remember this: "Call them when you miss them, but only panic when you hear a siren in the background." Your mama instincts will always be sharper than their Wi-Fi connection.

# SAYING "I FEEL MORE ALIVE NOW THAN I DID AT 30"... AND IT'S NOT EVEN A LIE

At 30, you were always on the move: happy hours, hangouts, weekends packed with friends, wrong boyfriends, and last-minute wax appointments. You smiled a lot—but slept very little.

And sometimes, the real question was: "Do I actually like this life... or am I just chasing the perfect mojito?" Now, at 60, waking up feels like a new episode of a show you actually want to watch. You spend your mornings thinking, "How can I spoil myself today?" The days of running on fumes for everyone else are gone.

So when you say, "I feel more alive now than I did at 30," no one should be surprised.
You've stopped pleasing everyone else and started choosing you.

And no, you don't need an aperitif to feel lit up inside —just a comfy couch, someone who really listens (even if it's you), and a '90s playlist.

## GOING OUT DANCING ON THE WEEKEND... EVEN IF IT'S JUST IN YOUR LIVING ROOM, WITH 1999 ENERGY

Once upon a time, weekends meant clubbing in high heels, sweating like you were running a marathon, and praying you'd make it home with mascara mostly in place.

Now? Saturday night finds you in your living room, barefoot, with your favorite 90's playlist and a cushioned floor to break your fall.
At 60, you don't dance to be seen—you dance because it feels amazing.
Because your body remembers every step, every move, every song.

And sometimes, if your back's feeling generous, you even throw in a spin—just like the good old days.
Who says fun has an age limit?
And if you ever doubt it, just remember: All you really need is a power strip, Spotify Premium, and a floor that doesn't make you wish you had a helmet.

# STOPPING THE ACT: NO MORE FAKING ENTHUSIASM FOR ENDLESS FAMILY LUNCHES

There was a time when you'd dress for these things and maybe even bring a smile with you. Now? You're checking your watch the moment you walk in. The family script is the same:

- Who's gossiping about what cousin did what?
- Who's talking too loudly?
- Who'll ask about your job like it's the first time ever?

At 60, you've run out of energy for extra forks, invasive questions, and never-ending meals you can't escape until the grappa hits the table. It's not that you don't love your family...

It's just that you'd rather see them in 20-minute episodes—with an intro theme and a "skip recap" button.

So you start pacing yourself:

You show up late with Zen-like calm.

You pretend to get a phone call.

You sit next to the one nice aunt (the only one).

And most of all... you start telling the truth when they ask, "Did you have a good time?"

# LETTING EVERYONE FEND FOR THEMSELVES AT DINNER

At 60, you realize you're no longer responsible for saving anyone from hunger. You're not the household chef, not a public cafeteria, and honestly—you're not even sure you're hungry yourself.

So one evening, you look around, do a quick calculation, and say out loud:
"Tonight, everyone's on their own."

(And you say it without guilt. In fact, with pride.)
You heat up a ready-made soup or eat two slices of cheese standing up, using a dessert fork.
The others? Pizza, cereal, bread, and tuna—or despair. Not your problem.

The real win isn't eating light or healthy.
It's not having to worry about what anyone else is eating while you dream of your couch and a show with nice, slow dialogue.

# TURNING READING GLASSES INTO A PERSONAL STYLE STATEMENT

At 60, you've learned that seeing things up close isn't a right—it's a full-on logistics operation.
You've got a pair in the kitchen, one on the nightstand, one in your bag, one in the car... And yet, every time you need to read something, none of them are anywhere to be found.

So, you start the signature routine:
Arms stretched out, lights cranked up, eyes locked in a showdown with the calorie label.
And eventually, you give in:
"Alexa, you read it."
The funny part? You're not actually losing your glasses. They're hiding.

Sometimes, they're on top of your head.
Other times... you're already wearing them.

# STOPPING THE BATTLE TO MAKE YOUR KIDS EAT VEGETABLES

You spent years crafting strategies: mashed veggie decoys, shredded zucchini, soups in disguise.

Every meal felt like a diplomatic mission between broccoli and the spoon.

Then, one day, you woke up and said:
"Let them eat what they want. I'm making myself a nice soup, and that's that."
At 60, you understand that peace of mind is worth more than a carrot eaten under protest.
And if your grown kid still insists on plain pasta with parmesan... that's their issue, not your failure.

You did your part. You cooked, explained, and even threatened a little.
Now you get to enjoy your colorful plate—and the joy of a table where no one's whining.

## 💡 BONUS TIP

Keep a line ready for when they say, "I don't feel like having salad": "Perfect. More for me. And I need the fiber."

# OWNING A MEDICINE CABINET THAT PUTS THE LOCAL PHARMACY TO SHAME

**64**

Band-aids in every size.
White pills, yellow ones, fizzy tablets, chewables.
Sprays, drops, ointments, miracle teas, and your aunt's remedies for every known illness (and a few made-up ones).
At 60, your home pharmacy is more organized than your actual closet.

You've got something for headaches, stomachaches, existential dread... and even for the dog, just in case.
If someone coughs in the house, you don't ask, "How are you feeling?" You ask, "Homeopathic or pharmaceutical?"
And the best part? You don't throw anything away.
That box of Tylenol from 2016? Still there.
Just in case.
(But you check the expiration date now and then—because you're responsible, too.)

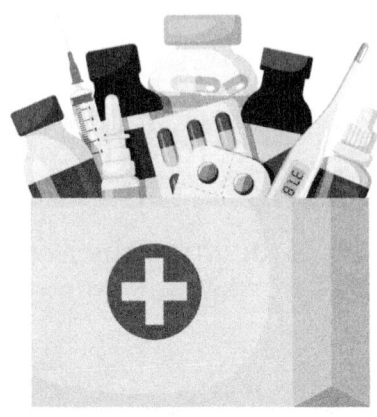

# SLEEPING IN THE UGLIEST, MOST COMFORTABLE PAJAMAS ON EARTH

Silk? Lace? Cute matching sets? No thanks.
At 60, fleece wins. Faded t-shirts, stretched-out pants with an elastic waistband that's
holding on out of sheer habit.
It's not laziness.

It's comfort, elevated to a life philosophy.
You've learned that sleeping well matters more than looking elegant on the journey from bed to fridge.
And if someone says, "Isn't that pajama set a little... sad?" You smile, wrap yourself in your soft cotton cocoon, and reply: "Maybe. But I sleep like royalty in it."

# LOOKING AT YOUR GROWN-UP KIDS AND THINKING: "I MUST'VE DONE SOMETHING RIGHT"

One's out having cocktail downtown, talking about mortgages.

The other corrects you on how to use tech properly.

And you just sit there, watching in silence, thinking: "Where did these humans even come from?"

At 60, seeing your kids as adults feels like tuning into a show where you somehow missed the last three seasons.

You recognize the features, the mannerisms—but now and then, you wonder if they were raised in a parallel project you forgot you were part of.

Then you remember that day you were trimming their nails while they screamed like you were sacrificing them.

And now they're discussing "long-term strategies."

The truth?

Yes, you raised them.

Even if sometimes... you're not quite sure how.

# TALKING TO YOURSELF

You ask a question—and answer it.
You comment on what's on TV, argue with the washing machine, and announce out
loud that you're leaving the room.
And the best part? No one argues back.

At 60, talking to yourself isn't a sign of losing it—it's a sign of mental clarity.
You need to hear yourself to understand yourself.
And let's be honest: some of your solo conversations are sharper than most dinner parties.

And if someone catches you deep in debate with your sock drawer?
Just smile and say:
"I'm in a staff meeting."

# SAYING "I DON'T KNOW HOW" JUST TO AVOID HAVING TO DO IT

They ask you to make a PDF, open a shared drive, or download yet another app just to book a table.
You smile vaguely, lift your reading glasses, and say: "Ugh... I'm terrible with this tech stuff."
At 60, you've mastered the art of the strategic boomer act.

You know perfectly well how to use a smartphone.
You can reset passwords, mute group chats, and even send a certified email if needed.
But not today.

And the best part? No one insists.
Because today, you're going full "I'm just not a tech person." With a pretty sincere tone, everyone believes you–and leave you alone.

## 💡 BONUS TIP

Use this move sparingly, and only with people who don't live with you.
Anyone who's seen you troubleshoot the printer while chatting with Alexa... won't fall for it again.

# READING A BOOK FOR HOURS

At 60, reading isn't just a hobby—it's mental self-preservation.

You open a book and disappear. Not to escape, but to find yourself.

You read in bed, on the couch, in the car while waiting for someone (who will, obviously, be late).

And it doesn't matter if it takes you three months to finish.

What matters is that those pages are yours alone.

You've discovered the joy of underlining a sentence just because it gave you chills. You find yourself rereading the same chapter because you drifted off in your thoughts—and honestly, that was a good chapter, too. And if someone calls you while you're reading? You pretend not to hear. You're in another world.

# REDISCOVERING THAT BENEATH "MOM AND DAD," THERE ARE STILL TWO PEOPLE IN LOVE

When the kids grow up and become independent, a new space opens up in your relationship.
You're no longer just "their parents"—you're back to being the two of you.

Two people who chose each other, loved each other, supported each other—even when everything revolved around the family. At sixty, there's finally time to look into each other's eyes without interruption. To rediscover the gestures, the glances, the silent connections that brought you together in the first place. The roles start to fade, and what's left is what really matters:

The closeness, the tenderness, the love that grew right alongside you. It's no longer about doing things out of obligation—but out of joy.
The pleasure of being together.
Of sharing a quiet coffee. Of laughing like you used to.
And you realize the spark is still there.
Only now, it glows warmer, wiser, and more real than ever.

# CREATING A PHOTO ALBUM JUST FOR YOU... AND FLIPPING THROUGH IT LIKE A GENTLE HUG

You don't need to post them. You don't even need them to be perfectly arranged. At 60, you make an album simply for the joy of having a place where moments stay. Crooked shots, blurry faces—but full of laughter. A trip that brought you back to life.

A dinner with someone who's no longer here.

A younger you, twenty years ago, with the same smile you wear today.

It's not nostalgia—it's tender memory.

It's telling yourself, "Look how much life I've already lived."

And maybe getting a little emotional... but with a full heart.

And every once in a while, you open it again.

Maybe with a cup of tea.

Maybe in silence.

Maybe with a song that takes you right back to that exact moment.

# WATCHING A MOVIE YOU KNOW WILL MAKE YOU CRY—IN THE BEST WAY

You know that movie you picked?
The one that pulls at your heartstrings, makes you ugly-cry, and somehow leaves you feeling a little lighter?

At 60, you don't avoid those strong emotions—you just welcome them.
Because you've learned that some tears aren't sadness... they're release.
And crying in your pajamas, blanket over your legs, face all red—that's one of the most honest things you can give yourself.

And if someone asks, "Why do you watch things that make you feel bad?" You answer,
"Because they make me feel better after."

## 💡 BONUS TIP

Always keep a "crying blanket" and a box of tissues close by.
(And a bar of chocolate. The heart has its needs.) If not for the movie, for the aftermath.

# RECONNECTING WITH OLD CLASSMATES—JUST OUT OF CURIOSITY

Finding an old classmate might seem like a nostalgic move, but really, it's a meaningful way to reflect on how far you've come.

You might not expect much from a simple conversation, but it can surprise you—reminding you how different you were back then and how much you've grown. Reaching out to an old friend is like watching a faded photo come to life. It's an excuse to stir up old memories.

It's not about rekindling a friendship—it's about sharing a quick "here's where I am now," laughing about who you used to be, and appreciating who you've become.

Plus, it's a great opportunity to explain your much more refined social media skills.

# REORGANIZING YOUR CLOSET WITH A "DONATE OR KEEP" MARATHON

You open the doors with courage. You pause. Take a breath.

Then the challenge begins: this stays, this goes, and this one... why do I even still have it?

At 60, cleaning out your closet isn't just a task–it's an emotional reckoning. You find clothes that no longer reflect who you are; others tied to memories you can now release with a smile.

And then there they are: the "when I have time to get back in shape" pants. Spoiler: you're already in shape –just a different one. And you're done punishing yourself with tight jeans.

And if you really want to avoid the whole mess, just leave it all for your kids to deal with in 30 years.

# LEAVING A GROUP CHAT—NO EXPLANATION, JUST PURE INNER PEACE

You used to stay "to be polite."
Now, after 237 messages in 24 hours about cakes, good morning memes, and chain messages, you tap "Leave Chat"... and smile.

At 60, you've learned you don't need to be everywhere.
Your time is sacred, silence isn't rude, and not replying doesn't make you unkind—it makes you healthier.
And if someone texts you privately:

"Why did you leave the group?"
You reply with the calm of a woman set free:
"Because I ran out of mental space. And patience, too."
And if they send a "sad face," just ignore it for a week and enjoy the peace.

# STARTING A COLLECTION OF SOMETHING YOU LOVE

At 60, it's the perfect time to dive into a passion that takes you on a little time-travel adventure– something that makes you feel youthful in spirit and opens new doors to curiosity. Starting a collection, whether it's stamps, old coins, vinyl records, or items from your childhood, is a unique way to gather pieces of history that speak directly to you.

It's not about accumulating stuff–it's about curating fragments of something you truly care about. Every item becomes a discovery, a story, and a chance to learn more about a topic that fascinates you. A collection can also be a great way to connect with others who share your passion.

Start slow, no pressure–just explore what draws you in.

## 💡 BONUS TIP

Here are a few ideas to spark your collection:
- Stamps or coins
- Rare books or first editions
- Vintage comic books
- Miniature perfumes
- Crystals and minerals
- Vintage photographs

# CARING FOR A PET—EVEN IF YOU THOUGHT IT WASN'T FOR YOU

"Allergic to fur."
"No time."
"Not my thing."
Then they showed up—with sweet eyes, wobbly paws, or a bold little meow.
And now you talk to them. In baby talk. Shamelessly.
At 60, you've discovered that a pet doesn't just fill your house—it opens your heart.
Sometimes, all it takes is a wagging tail or a loud purr to save your whole day.
And even if you swore you wouldn't leave the house looking a mess... you do. Because "I have to take them out."
You find yourself buying treats, pillows, toys, and tiny sweaters.
And you'll never admit it, but yes—
you talk to them like they're your kid.
And they answer you.
With their eyes.

# LEARNING TO STAY SILENT... AND FEELING LIKE THE MOST POWERFUL ONE IN THE ROOM

You used to respond to everything.
You defended, explained, argued, justified.

Now you listen. You assess. And then you decide if it's even worth replying. (Spoiler: it rarely is.)
At 60, you've learned that silence isn't emptiness—it's discernment.
Choosing not to jump into a pointless argument is an act of self-respect.
Refusing to gossip doesn't make you boring—it makes you free.

And when you stay quiet, the people who really know you can hear everything you're saying.
With a glance. With a pause. With the grace of someone who no longer needs to prove anything.

# PLANNING A REUNION WITH OLD FRIENDS

**79**

At 60, friendships from the past hit differently—and getting together with old friends feels like reopening a chapter you thought was long closed.

Planning a reunion with your childhood or school friends is one of the most joyful things you can do. The laughs, the memories, the stories from your younger years—those never get old.

But more than anything, seeing how they've changed too, and realizing that despite the years, there's still that special connection only true friendships hold onto.

You catch up, share hilarious old stories, and laugh about the things that once felt huge but now just make you smile with wisdom.

It's not just a reunion—it's a return to your roots. A rediscovery of who you were, who you are now, and how far you've come.

At 60, these friendships are treasures. And moments like this are how you keep them shining.

# CHOOSE YOUR BRA BASED ON COMFORT.

You used to go for lace, push-ups, and gravity-defying balconettes.
Now you want wide straps, no wires, and a soft hug that doesn't leave marks.
At 60, your bra isn't a tool of seduction—it's a peace treaty.

If you wear one, it has to be an ally.
And if you can skip it? Even better.

Because you've discovered that real freedom is getting home, unhooking it with one hand like a ninja, and feeling like you just shed ten years of social pressure.

## 💡 BONUS TIP

You know who loves this new freedom even more than you do?
Your husband. Surprise, No bra? He thinks you've never looked sexier.
(And you can't help but laugh. But the look he gives you says it all.)

# WALK INTO A FAST FOOD JOINT... AND ORDER WHATEVER THE HELL YOU WANT.

**81**

You used to sneak in, say, "Just a little salad, I'm on a diet," then swipe fries off someone else's tray.
Now?

You walk in like you own the place, order exactly what you're craving, ask for extra mayo... and sit down like someone who just made peace with the universe.
At 60, you've learned that fast food, once in a while, is a joy—not a crime.

And if someone gives you the stink eye while you chew your cheeseburger in peace?
Ignore them. They're probably just mad they didn't order fries, too.

# HEAR SOMEONE SAY, "WOMEN DRIVERS..." AND THEN PARK BETTER THAN THEY EVER COULD.

All it took was one look.

You pulled a U-turn in a space that looked impossible, backed in with surgical precision, and shut off the engine like someone who just crushed a stereotype without saying a word.

At 60, you don't need anyone telling you how to drive.

You don't ask, "Can you come with me?"
And if the car needs to go far—you're the one taking it there.

You've driven with screaming kids, overpacked trunks, pouring rain, a glitchy GPS, and a 3% battery. And guess what? You always made it.

# WATCH TWENTY-SOMETHINGS AND THINK, "POOR THINGS, THEY HAVE NO IDEA YET."

You see them rushing around, second-guessing everything, spiraling over an unread text.

They're in a hurry to figure it all out, terrified of making the wrong move, convinced every decision is forever.

And you, at 60, just smile: "Poor things, they have no idea yet." It's not arrogance—it's experience.

It's knowing that breakdowns pass, mistakes teach, and life doesn't follow a perfect script.

That real love is often the one that stays, not the one that sweeps you off your feet.

That you're not defined by your job or the number of likes you get.

You've been through it. You've cried, fought, feared.

And now, with a few more lines on your face and a lot more lightness in your heart, you've learned that real strength is letting go of control. At 60, you can listen without judging.

You can simply say, "It'll pass."

And mean it.

Because every storm calms down eventually. And life, surprisingly, really does get better. Your birth year? A stylish little mystery.

"What year were you born?"

"Good question."

# GOING TO BED AT 9 P.M. NO EXCUSES. JUST BECAUSE IT FEELS GOOD.

You're not tired.
You're not sick.
You don't have a headache.

You just want to slip into your pajamas by 8:30, crawl into fresh sheets, turn off the world... and smile.
At 60, you've realized it's not boredom—it's peace.
Going to bed early is a classy move.

And no happy hour can compete with that moment you sink into your comforter while everyone else is still deciding where to eat.

## 💡 BONUS TIP

Turn your "early night" into a sacred ritual:
Herbal tea, moisturizing cream, zero notifications, and maybe one episode of your favorite show (that you won't finish—because tonight, you're happily out cold).

## PUTTING FEWER CANDLES ON THE CAKE

At 60, you don't count the years anymore. You count wishes. Maybe calories—if you feel like it.
Candles? Two are enough: one for "sixty" and one for "don't care." (Or just one symbolic
spark. Even better: a little sparkler and done.)

Because if you tried putting them all on, you'd need:

- A cake the size of a tennis court
- A fan to blow them out
- A fire extinguisher, just in case

At this point in life, the real flame is yours. And no puff of air can blow that out. Not even a hurricane-force breeze.

# DONATING TO A CAUSE YOU CARE ABOUT

At 60, you realize you can't change the whole world—but you can make a difference. Even with a small gesture. Even quietly. A donation, no matter how modest, made from the heart, becomes something that warms you, gives you purpose, and connects you to something bigger.

Whether it's to support women in need, animals, children, or the environment, you're not doing it to be seen. You're doing it to stay true to who you've become. Because the real luxury now is being able to give.

It's not about how much—it's about why. It's your way of saying, "I'm here." And afterward, you feel better. Not out of duty, but because it feels right.

It's also an example. A seed that might inspire someone watching. A way to leave a mark. Maybe it's the start of something bigger—or maybe not. But it'll be yours. And it'll be beautiful.

# HOSTING A GAME NIGHT WITH FRIENDS OR FAMILY

Who says having fun has to mean crowded bars and noisy nights out? At 60, you can rediscover the joy of a simple evening at home–with board games, snacks, a cup of tea or a glass of wine, and the kind of people who make you feel good.

You don't need to be the perfect hostess. Just a casually set table and a few games– Taboo, Clue, Monopoly, Dixit... or Pictionary if you're in the mood to laugh till you cry. It's not about winning. It's about connecting. About making eye contact, laughing for real, unplugging from the screens, and being present.

Playing is a little act of rebellion–it's proof you haven't forgotten how to have fun, that you still know how to not take yourself too seriously. And when the night ends with crumbs on the table and laughter still hanging in the air, you think: we should do this more often. And yes, you can–because now, there's no need to drive home.

## LEARNING TO BAKE BREAD AND ENJOYING IT FRESH FROM THE OVEN

Flour everywhere, dough-covered hands, the timer going off...

And then that smell fills the house, a reminder of simple joys and quiet satisfaction.

At 60, baking bread isn't a trend—it's a declaration of independence.

You don't just buy—you create.

You don't tear open a package—you knead, you wait, you honor the process.

And when you finally pull it from the oven—warm, fragrant, imperfect, and beautiful—you realize you're not just eating. You're celebrating yourself.

And you have to admit, it's a little thrilling to know you've got bread that rivals the bakery. But also, now you're officially "the person who bakes bread."

# MEETING A GROUP OF TEENAGERS AND INSTANTLY COMPARING THEM TO "HOW YOU WERE AT THEIR AGE."

You see them: wild haircuts, baggy pants, earbuds in, already tired faces on a Monday morning.
And that little voice inside you speaks up:

"At their age, I..."
- woke up without back pain
- left the house without a phone
- knew how to have fun without apps
- and above all... even in low-rise jeans, I had more style.

It's not envy. It's a quiet comparison, with a built-in sense of satisfaction. Because sure, maybe you had fewer things... but everything felt more real, more intense, more alive. And if you find yourself smiling as they film TikToks in the middle of the street, just think: "You're adorable. But at your age... I really danced."

## 💡 BONUS TIP

When someone asks if you feel old when you see younger people, say: "No, I feel lucky. I've already lived it. They're still on their way."

## VISITING YOUR KIDS WHO (FINALLY) LIVE ON THEIR OWN... AND LEAVING WITH A FULL LOAD OF LAUNDRY

You stopped by just for a coffee.
"Don't worry, Mom, everything's under control."
Then you opened the bathroom door and found:
A damp towel from 2019, six lonely socks, and a pile of t-shirts crying for help.

At 60, even if your kids live on their own, your washing machine still works overtime for them.
They say, "I've got this," but you end up driving home with a laundry bag that looks like it came from a rugby team.

And sure, they won't admit it—but that clean, home-washed smell has magic in it.
Kind of like you.

# TIDYING UP YOUR MEMORIES NOT JUST YOUR DRAWERS

At 60, you're not just organizing sweaters and expired paperwork.
Then, you open a box and find a photo, a letter, or even a train ticket. You might not remember where it was headed, but you remember exactly how it made you feel.

So you start to tidy up.
Let go of what weighs you down; hold onto what warms you up.
You realize some memories no longer serve you—others deserve a brand-new frame.
It's not nostalgia.

It's emotional decluttering.
A way to make space for the present, without throwing the past away.

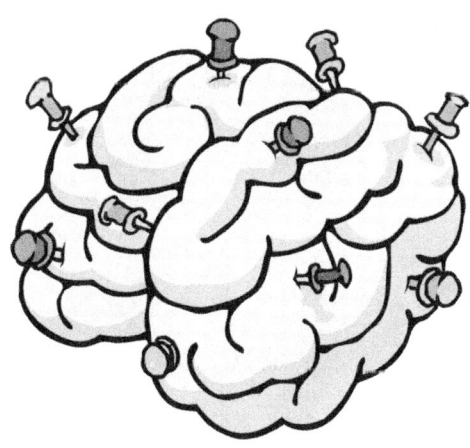

# NO LONGER GETTING OFFENDED BY EVERYTHING... AND SAVING YOUR ENERGY FOR MORE IMPORTANT THINGS (LIKE PICKING THE RIGHT WINE)

At 60, you realize not everything deserves a reaction, an explanation, or a sulk.

They forgot to say goodbye? Oh well.

They interrupted you mid-sentence? How original.

They said, "You don't look your age"? Smile, say thanks... and think, "You know where you can put that opinion."

You've learned that true elegance is letting things go.

Not because you don't care—but because you've stopped stressing just for sport.

Now you save your energy for what really matters:

A good book, dinner with someone who makes you laugh, and a whole day where your phone doesn't ring once.

## ACCEPTING THAT YOUR CHILD DOESN'T THINK LIKE YOU

They look you in the eye and say something you never would've said at their age.

Different ideas, different dreams–maybe even choices you just don't get.
And for a moment, you want to say, "Okay, but listen to your mother..."
Then you breathe.

And remember: you raised them this way.
Free to think, to choose, to make mistakes.
(Even if saying it out loud is still a weekly workout.)
At 60, you understand that real love isn't making them think like you– it's standing by them even when they go in the opposite direction. And if you really can't help yourself?
Write what you want to say in a note on your phone.
Then delete it.
It's therapeutic. And quiet.

# SAYING, "I'M NOT COOKING TODAY—WE'RE EATING WHATEVER'S THERE."

There was a time you scrambled to make "something nice for everyone." Now, you open the fridge, assess your remaining energy, and calmly declare: "I'm not cooking today. We're eating whatever's there." It's a simple phrase—but a powerful one.

It means I'm not sacrificing myself today; I'm not in the mood for pots and pans, and that's perfectly fine.
Who's hungry, will find something.
Who's picky, will figure it out.

And you? You enjoy a meal with no dishes to wash and a quiet sense of triumph.
Because at 60, true five-star dining means freedom.

# REVISITING AN OLD DREAM AND SEEING IF YOU'RE READY NOW

Maybe you set it aside years ago.
Not enough time, not enough money, not enough courage... or just life pulling you in another direction.
But now, that dream is knocking again. Softly–but firmly.

At 60, you have something you didn't before: experience, clarity, and way less fear of what people think.
Maybe you don't need to go big–maybe starting is enough. Even small. Even just for you.
Writing that book. Learning to dance (again). Opening a tiny shop that sells... what exactly? You don't know yet, but "it's going to be BIG."
Visiting that place. Taking that class. Saying, "Why not?"

Because maybe it's not too late.
Maybe... it's exactly the right time.

Write it down. On paper, in your phone, on your mirror: "It's not a forgotten dream. It's just running late."

# STARTING A HERB GARDEN ON YOUR BALCONY—BECAUSE MAYBE YOUR GREEN THUMB JUST NEEDED TIME

**96**

At 60, your green thumb might finally be blooming—even if you never thought plant care was your thing.

Creating a small herb garden on your balcony is the perfect way to connect with nature, even in a tiny space. It becomes a little patch of beauty at home—and bonus: you can use the herbs to flavor your cooking.

Growing rosemary, basil, mint, or thyme is a soothing activity that lets you care for something without the pressure to get it all "just right." Every sprouting leaf feels like a quiet win.

It's the perfect time to try something new—something that blends peace, purpose, and the joy of growing things with your own hands.

P.S. You will feel proud when you tell your friends that you "grew this basil yourself."

## LEARNING A NEW LANGUAGE— MAYBE THIS TIME YOU'LL FINALLY GO TO LONDON WITHOUT RELYING ON HAND GESTURES

**97**

At 60, you've got a lifetime of experience that helps you take on new challenges with the right mindset.

Learning a new language is exciting–it stimulates your brain and makes travel feel more real and more personal.

Maybe you've always dreamed of going to London, but ended up speaking with your hands.

Now, learning English–or any language–lets you connect with the world in a whole new way.

At this age, there's no pressure to be perfect. You're learning just for the joy of it. And the moment you understand a full conversation in another language? Pure magic.

Start small–with an online course or an app. It's never too late to speak the world's language. (And hey, now you'll know exactly what they're saying when they finally ask if you want your tea with milk.)

# BEING CALLED A "BOOMER"... AND TAKING IT AS A COMPLIMENT (SORT OF)

They call you "boomer" because you don't use TikTok, you text with punctuation, or you
ask, "Wait, what's BeReal?"
You just smile and think:

"I watched the internet being born, made mixtapes on cassettes, and survived 160-character texts. Boomer? Please."
At 60, being a boomer means having historical memory, top-tier sarcasm, and the glorious freedom of not caring what's considered "cringe" today. You've got your own way of doing things—and it works.

You lived before tutorials, filters, and spoiler warnings.

And guess what? You're still doing just fine.

## 💡 BONUS TIP

When someone jokingly calls you a boomer, respond with a calm smile and a little style: "Boomer? Absolutely. I've got retirement in sight and zero social anxiety. Who's really winning here?"

# TRYING A NEW HAIRSTYLE

At 60, you're not just cutting your hair. You're cutting off an era.

A new hairstyle isn't a whim—it's a declaration of freedom:

"I want to see myself differently. I want to feel new. And maybe try some bangs; why not."
You look in the mirror at a style you've never had before and think, "Hmm... I'll need time to get used to this." Five minutes later:
"Wait... I kinda love it."
Ten minutes later: selfie. From every angle. With the "casual but fabulous" filter, of course.
And if someone says, "You look different,"
you smile and reply:
"I am. And not just my hair."

# WEARING SUNGLASSES EVEN WHEN THERE'S NO SUN

At sixty, you've finally earned the right to do things just because you feel like it. And sunglasses? They're the perfect example.

Why wait for full sunshine to wear them? Throw them on when the sky is gray, when it's raining, even indoors if you're feeling a little extra. Because, let's face it—sunglasses are magic.

They hide dark circles, fine lines, tired eyes... and just as importantly, they make you feel instantly cooler.

They give you that mysterious edge, that bold elegance of someone who's realized she doesn't need a reason to be herself.

You don't owe anyone an explanation for your choices.

So, if you're feeling chic, playful, or just not in the mood for makeup—put them on.

Round, square, vintage, modern—wear them like you mean it.

And rock that "I look amazing and don't need to prove it" energy.

Plus, nobody really asks why. They just nod and keep moving.

# BEING ALONE... AND FEELING NO NEED TO EXPLAIN YOURSELF

Back then, spending an evening alone meant coming up with excuses: "I'm just tired," "Didn't feel like it," "Plans fell through." Now, you simply say: "Tonight, it's just me. And that's enough."

At 60, you've learned that silence isn't boring–it's peaceful. That not replying to messages isn't rude–it's energetic self-defense. That the couch, a warm tea, and a good book beat any night of small talk. You're not missing anything.

In fact, you finally have it all: time, space, and the freedom to choose who (not) to be with.

Printed in Dunstable, United Kingdom